AF784699

# CONTENTS

# STOLEN PASSPORTS: A TERRORIST'S FIRST CLASS TICKET

## HEARING

BEFORE THE

## COMMITTEE ON INTERNATIONAL RELATIONS HOUSE OF REPRESENTATIVES

ONE HUNDRED EIGHTH CONGRESS

SECOND SESSION

JUNE 23, 2004

**Serial No. 108–117**

Printed for the use of the Committee on International Relations

Available via the World Wide Web: http://www.house.gov/international_relations

U.S. GOVERNMENT PRINTING OFFICE

94–508PDF WASHINGTON : 2004

For sale by the Superintendent of Documents, U.S. Government Printing Office
Internet: bookstore.gpo.gov Phone: toll free (866) 512–1800; DC area (202) 512–1800
Fax: (202) 512–2250 Mail: Stop SSOP, Washington, DC 20402–0001

## COMMITTEE ON INTERNATIONAL RELATIONS

# STOLEN PASSPORTS: A TERRORIST'S FIRST CLASS TICKET

---

**WEDNESDAY, JUNE 23, 2004**

HOUSE OF REPRESENTATIVES,
COMMITTEE ON INTERNATIONAL RELATIONS,
*Washington, DC.*

The Committee met, pursuant to call, at 10:34 a.m. In Room 2172, Rayburn House Office Building, Hon. Henry J. Hyde (Chairman of the Committee) presiding.

Chairman HYDE. The Committee will come to order.

I want to thank our witnesses for agreeing to be on our panel today. I know protocol is very important, but everybody has a full plate today, and we appreciate your cooperation.

In today's world, when countries are tightening up their border controls due to terrorism concerns, what could be more valuable than a first class ticket to travel anywhere in the world? A stolen passport may be worth more than its weight in gold.

As we will hear today, travel document fraud represents a growing concern of law enforcement around the world. Certainly, here in the U.S., it is viewed as a serious threat to national security.

Last month, the State Department announced a new program that would contribute to the security of our Nation. The U.S. will now participate in Interpol's stolen document database, which is available to border authorities worldwide. Not only will this sharing of vital information curb the movements of organized criminals and terrorists, but it will significantly reduce identity theft problems, as well. We laud the efforts of Interpol in taking the initiative by assembling a very useful tool to be used by the international community. I believe it will substantially contribute to the level of security that all nations desire to achieve.

I look forward to hearing the testimony of our witnesses today in order to gauge the level of a problem which exists both in the U.S. and on a worldwide basis, and to assess our efforts in curbing the theft of travel documents.

I am now pleased to yield to my friend and colleague, Ranking Member Mr. Lantos, for any opening remarks he may choose to make.

[The prepared statement of Mr. Hyde follows:]

PREPARED STATEMENT OF THE HONORABLE HENRY J. HYDE, A REPRESENTATIVE IN CONGRESS FROM THE STATE OF ILLINOIS, AND CHAIRMAN, COMMITTEE ON INTERNATIONAL RELATIONS

In today's world when countries are tightening up their border controls due to terrorism concerns, what could be more valuable than a first-class ticket to travel unfettered anywhere in the world? A stolen passport may be worth *more* than its weight in gold.

As we will hear today, travel document fraud represents a growing concern to law enforcement authorities around the world. Certainly, here in the United States, it may be viewed as a serious threat to national security.

Last month, the U.S. State Department announced a new program that would contribute to the security of our nation. The United States will now participate in Interpol's stolen document database, which is available to border authorities worldwide. Not only will this sharing of vital information curb the movement of organized criminals and terrorists, but it will significantly reduce identity theft problems, as well. We laud the efforts of Interpol in taking the initiative by assembling a very useful tool to be used by the international community. I believe it will substantially contribute to the level of security that all nations desire to achieve.

I look forward to hearing the testimony of our witnesses today in order to gauge the level of a problem which exists both here in the United States and on a worldwide basis, and to assess our efforts in curbing the theft of travel documents.

I will now yield to my friend and colleague, Ranking Democratic Member Tom Lantos, for any opening remarks he may wish to make.

Mr. LANTOS. Thank you very much, Mr. Chairman.

First, let me commend you on convening this very important hearing. It is crucial that Congress call attention to the growing problem of stolen passports as it represents a serious national security threat. How serious? We really do not know, because there is no precise way to track passports that are stolen abroad even as they are used to cross our own borders.

Tens of thousands of these documents are stolen each year in visa waiver countries, those countries whose passport holders are not required to obtain visas for visits of less than 90 days to the United States. So whoever gets his hands on these passports by any means has a free and easy entry into this country; and although Interpol has recently launched a database of stolen passport numbers, there evidently is a crippling lack of coordination between the U.S. Department of Homeland Security and Interpol on this point.

I am concerned, Mr. Chairman, that the United States government is not doing enough to ensure worldwide passport security, particularly with respect to countries that qualify for the Visa Waiver Program. For example, in France, over the last year, more than 14,000 French passports were stolen by the truckload in three separate instances. One of them showed up in the hands of an Algerian who reportedly was stopped at JFK Airport only because the name of his traveling companion was on a law enforcement watch list.

Some 25,000 Canadian passports have also disappeared. Intelligence officials have reported that 80,000 blank passports have been stolen from 36 countries in recent years, among them Italy, Germany and Sweden. The numbers stolen in other countries could well be staggering. We understand that as many as 627,000 blank passports are lost or stolen in other countries, with as many as 75,000 in countries participating in the Visa Waiver Program.

It is no stretch of the imagination to suggest that this could be an attractive means for terrorists to enter into the United States. Trade in stolen travel documents is also a potentially lucrative way for terrorist groups to finance their operations.

Mr. Chairman, I am not encouraged that our own government's efforts to meet this threat are adequate. The Department of Homeland Security Inspector General reported this past April that the

Department does not have in place a process to check information on lost and stolen passports and other travel information that it receives from other countries against U.S. entry and exit statistics. Therefore, Homeland Security does not know the scope of the problem. We to not know the number of such documents that may still be in circulation, and it is unclear whether those we know of are even recorded in U.S. databases used to alert Border and Customs officials.

I am very pleased that the United States has recently decided to join Interpol's stolen travel documents database and to make available to Interpol the information about U.S. lost and stolen passports. My chief concern is that this cooperation is still too limited to be of much use. U.S. border control officers will not have immediate, real-time desktop access to Interpol's database. An incoming traveler's passport is referred for secondary investigation which includes an Interpol check only if a border control inspector at the point of entry has reason to suspect that traveler of wrongdoing.

For the Interpol database to be useful to us or any other country targeted by terrorists for infiltration, border control officials must have the capability to determine immediately whether a passport presented to them is in the database. Relying on all our officers to have some innate sense that something is amiss after they have seen and processed hundreds of people every day is clearly not enough. I hope our witnesses today will concentrate their remarks on this issue. What is required to get real-time access to this information? Does Interpol itself need to increase its capacity? Do the state members of Interpol need to provide more resources to accomplish this?

I look forward to hearing from our witnesses; and I thank you, Mr. Chairman.

Chairman HYDE. Thank you, Mr. Lantos.

The Chair will entertain brief opening statements.

Mr. Sherman.

Mr. SHERMAN. Thank you, Mr. Chairman.

I just arrived from the Financial Services Committee where when we say visa we mean a completely different document, that is to say, a credit card.

I would say the private sector has done a much better job in creating a document that is difficult to forge and easier to track when it has been forged or stolen then has the State Department. We as a society are serious that nobody is going to be able to get a TV set for free, and that is why we have so many security devices built into a credit card. By comparison, our travel documents are wanting. We need, of course, tamper-proof, we need forge-proof, we need to make sure that when a passport is created it has a nonchangeable, electronically readable number on it. Once it is reported stolen, or whether it is before or after it is used to create an individual passport for an identified person, that it is on a numeric list.

I would point out that we as a Congress took some heat by telling our visa waiver partners they had to have biometric passports, and it is my understanding that Japan and Britain took us seriously and actually could have met the deadline. Our State Department apparently was less skilled, or took us less seriously, and could not. That is why Congress gave an extension for 1 year or

2 years, creating the kind of security at our border that is created at every McDonald's when you go to buy a hamburger with a credit card.

Our Subcommittee on Terrorism and Proliferation had hearings on the biometric program that were, I believe, similar in legislative import to these hearings. So we will be told again why it cannot be done, why it cannot be done now and why the terrorists should get another 6 months or another year or another 2 years to exploit inadequate border control program.

I yield back.

Chairman HYDE. Mr. Tancredo.

Mr. TANCREDO. Mr. Chairman, I am very interested to get into the witnesses, so I will forego any opening comment.

Chairman HYDE. Thank you, sir.

Ms. Berkley.

Ms. BERKLEY. I have no opening statement.

Chairman HYDE. Mr. Pitts.

Mr. PITTS. I will pass.

Chairman HYDE. Thank you, Mr. Pitts.

Mrs. Davis.

Mrs. DAVIS. No opening.

Chairman HYDE. Thank you.

Clark Kent Ervin is the Inspector General of the United States Department of Homeland Security. Prior to his current post, Mr. Ervin served as the Inspector General of the United States Department of State and the Broadcasting Board of Governors. He also held various positions in the Texas State government, such as Assistant Secretary of State and Deputy Attorney General.

Mr. Ervin graduated with honors from Harvard College in 1980 with a Bachelor of Arts degree in Government. He then continued his studies at Oxford University as a Rhodes Scholar, earning a Master's Degree in 1982 before returning to Harvard Law School for his Doctor of Laws degree in 1985.

Mr. Frank E. Moss is the Deputy Secretary for Passport Services of the Bureau of Consular Affairs of the Department of State, where he is responsible for managing the production of passports for over 7 million American customers each year. From 1998 to 2003, Mr. Moss served as the Executive Director of the Bureau of Consular Affairs for the Department of State.

He graduated with honors from Georgetown University in 1974, holds a Master's in Public Administration from the Maxwell School of Citizenship and Public Affairs at Syracuse University. Mr. Moss is also a Distinguished Graduate and has a Master's Degree in National Resource Strategy from the Industrial College of the Armed Services at the National Defense University.

Mr. James M. Sullivan is the Director of the International Criminal Police Organization Interpol–U.S. National Central Bureau, as well as a career senior executive with the U.S. Marshals Service. Before his current assignment, Mr. Sullivan was the U.S. National Central Bureau Deputy Director.

He attended Northeastern University for Business Management and Bunker Hill College for Fire Science and Technology.

We are honored to have all of you appear before the Committee today.

Mr. Ervin, if you would provide us with a 5-minute summary of your statement. Your full statement will be made a part of the record.

## STATEMENT OF THE HONORABLE CLARK KENT ERVIN, INSPECTOR GENERAL, U.S. DEPARTMENT OF HOMELAND SECURITY

Mr. ERVIN. Thank you, Mr. Chairman, Mr. Lantos and Members of the Committee. I am pleased to have this opportunity to appear before you today to discuss the findings of my office's recent review of the security implications of the Visa Waiver Program and the threat that stolen passports pose to that program and, more broadly, to national security.

As you know, the Visa Waiver Program began as a pilot in 1986 and is now a permanent program that enables citizens from 27 countries to travel to the United States for tourism or business purposes for 90 days or less without obtaining a visa.

From the beginning, the program involved a balancing of security risks and benefits to commerce, tourism, foreign relations and the workload of the Department of State. Virtually all of those familiar with the Visa Waiver Program told us that the lost and stolen passport problem is the greatest security vulnerability associated with it. Our country is vulnerable because gaps in our treatment of lost or stolen passports remain.

To be specific, DHS does not have a formalized process to check lost and stolen passport information against entry and exit information to determine the scope of fraudulent visa waiver passports or to determine when a traveler overstays and does not leave the country as required.

Also, there are problems with how the United States obtains lost and stolen passport information and a need for more regularized collection of such information.

There are significant variations in security practices and internal control that foreign countries apply to their passport manufacturing and issuing processes which should be taken into account when DHS conducts the country reviews that assess a country's continued eligibility to participate in the Visa Waiver Program.

Even when lost and stolen passport data is properly reported to the United States and entered into our lookout systems, some passports reported as stolen may still be used to enter the United States.

In cases where inspectors identify stolen visa waiver country passports, the fraudulent documents frequently are returned to the travelers so they may use them to return to their country of origin.

Finally, a lack of training hampers inspectors' efforts to detect passport fraud.

Our report contained 14 recommendations for corrective action; and subsequent to the issuance of our report, the applicable DHS directorate, Border and Transportation Security, has responded and agreed to take corrective action in response to each recommendation.

One of the most significant corrective actions responsive to our report is the processing of visa waiver travelers through the United States Visitor and Immigration Status Indicator Technology, commonly known as US–VISIT. As implemented in December, 2003, US–VISIT excluded visa waiver travelers from its scope. We strongly recommended that visa waiver travelers be added to the US–VISIT program because of the additional screening, identification, and exit control features it offers.

On April 21, Secretary Ridge announced that BTS would begin to process visa waiver travelers through US–VISIT by September 30 of this year.

A second concern noted in our report was the ill-defined process by which a country's stolen and lost passport information is reported and disseminated among other countries. We are therefore pleased to learn of the Interpol plan to expand and regularize the reporting of lost and stolen passports. This initiative, when fully implemented and when all nations participate, should be of great benefit by permitting automatic checking at the port of entry to determine whether the traveler is presenting a lost or stolen passport.

Even with the completion of the corrective actions we have recommended, the Visa Waiver Program will always pose some security risk. During the course of our review, we obtained documents that recount instances in which blank, bona fide passports from other countries were stolen and, as determined from their serial numbers, later used to enter the United States, sometimes on multiple occasions. In some instances, entry was permitted even after the stolen passport has been posted in the lookout system.

On the basis of this information, I have asked my Office of Inspections to begin an examination of stolen passport usage. I cannot comment, of course, on ongoing work, but I can advise you that the review has obtained additional documentation that, while still subject to further analysis, strongly suggests that stolen passports can be used successfully to enter the United States today. I will report to you on the results of that review as soon as I am able.

With that, thank you very much.

Chairman HYDE. Thank you, and we surely look forward to that report.

[The prepared statement of Mr. Ervin follows:]

PREPARED STATEMENT OF THE HONORABLE CLARK KENT ERVIN, INSPECTOR GENERAL, U.S. DEPARTMENT OF HOMELAND SECURITY

Mr. Chairman, Ranking Member Lantos, and Members of the Committee,

I am pleased to have the opportunity to appear before you today to discuss the findings of my office's recent review of the visa waiver program and the threat that stolen passports pose to that program and more broadly, national security.

In April 2004, my office issued an inspection report, *An Evaluation of the Security Implications of the Visa Waiver Program*. Copies of the report have been provided to the Committee and are available to the public on our website.

The Visa Waiver Program began as a pilot program in 1986 and has evolved into a permanent program in which 27 nations participate. The program enables most citizens of these countries to travel to the United States for tourism or business purposes for 90 days or less without obtaining a visa.

From the beginning, the program involved a balancing of security risks and benefits to commerce, tourism, foreign relations, and the workload of the Department of State (DOS). Until the Department of Homeland Security (DHS) was established, immigration policy and the conduct of the visa waiver program were the responsibility of the Immigration and Naturalization Service of the Department of Justice (DOJ).

The visa waiver program has been studied before. The DOJ Office of the Inspector General (OIG) examined the visa waiver program in 1999 and in a follow-up report in 2002.[1] The reports recounted timeliness and accuracy problems when stolen passport data was entered into lookout systems, failures to check lookout systems when passports were presented, and disorder in the management of the stolen passport program. More recently in November 2002, the General Accounting Office considered whether the visa waiver program should be ended, but did not recommend elimination.[2] My office undertook to look carefully at security issues in the visa waiver program and make recommendations to strengthen its management, focus and procedures now that DHS is established and largely responsible for the program.

Virtually all those familiar with the visa waiver program told us that the lost and stolen passport problem is the greatest security problem associated with the visa waiver program. Our country is vulnerable because gaps in our treatment of lost and stolen passports remain. To be specific:

- DHS does not have a process to check lost and stolen passport information against entry and exit information to determine the scope of fraudulent use of visa waiver passports, or to determine when a traveler overstays and does not leave the country as required.
- There continue to be problems with how the United States obtains lost and stolen passport information from visa waiver program participating governments and a need for a more regularized collection of such information. In at least one foreign country visited during our fieldwork, we observed substantial uncertainty over how to report thefts of its passports to our country.
- There are significant variations in the security practices and internal controls that foreign countries apply to their passport manufacturing and issuing processes. We urged that DHS examine these passport controls when it conducts the country reviews that assess a country's continued eligibility to participate in the visa waiver program.
- Even when lost and stolen passport data is properly reported to the U.S. and entered into U.S. lookout systems, some passports reported as stolen may still be used to enter the United States. We have indications that stolen passports have been used to enter the United States, even after September 11, 2001.
- In cases where inspectors identify stolen VWP passports presented by applicants who are denied entry, the fraudulent documents frequently are returned so that the travelers may use them to return to their country of origin.
- We also reported that a lack of training hampers POE inspectors' efforts to detect VWP passport fraud.

Many of the problems we encountered during this review are either the same as the earlier reported problems or closely related to them. Our report contained 14 recommendations for corrective action in response to the vulnerabilities we observed in the program. Subsequent to the issuance of our report, the Border and Transportation Security (BTS) directorate has responded to our report and agreed to take corrective action in response to each recommendation.

One of the most significant corrective actions responsive to the concerns stated in our report is the processing of visa waiver travelers through US Visitor and Immigrant Status Indicator Technology (US–VISIT). As implemented in December 2003, US–VISIT excluded visa waiver travelers from its scope. We strongly recommended that visa waiver travelers be added to the US–VISIT program because of the additional screening, identification, and exit control features it offers. On April 21, 2004, DHS Secretary Ridge announced that BTS would begin to process visa waiver travelers through US–VISIT ". . . by September 30, 2004."

A second and equally important concern from our report was the ill-defined process by which information about a country's stolen and lost passports are reported and disseminated among other countries. We are therefore pleased to learn of the INTERPOL plan to consolidate and regularize reporting of lost and stolen passports. This initiative, when fully implemented and when all nations participate, should be of great benefit by permitting automatic checking at the checkpoint or port of entry of whether the traveler is presenting a lost or stolen passport.

Even with the completion of the corrective actions we recommended, the visa waiver program will always pose some security risk. The fundamental premise of the program is that millions of persons, about whom we know little, can be exempt-

---

[1] *The Potential for Fraud and INS's Efforts to Reduce the Risks of the Visa Waiver Pilot Program*, Report No. I–99–10 (Mar. 1999); *Follow-up Report on the Visa Waiver Program*, Report No. I–2002–002 (Dec. 2001).

[2] *Border Security: Implications of Eliminating the Visa Waiver Program*, GAO–03–38 (Nov. 22, 2002).

ed from DOS' ever more rigorous visa procedures and permitted to board U.S.-bound planes. As we said in our report, "The visa is more than a mere stamp in a passport. It is the end result of a rigorous screening process the bearer must undergo before travel." By the end of the visa interview DOS has collected and stored considerable information about the traveler and the traveler's planned journey. DOS has introduced biometric features into its visas, shares data from its visa records with DHS port of entry systems, and significantly increased the percentage of applicants subject to a careful interview. In contrast, the visa waiver traveler is interviewed briefly, and the passport examined, again briefly by an inspector who may be unfamiliar with even valid passports from the issuing country.

During the course of our review of the visa waiver program, we obtained documents that recount instances in which blank, bona fide passports from other countries were stolen and, as determined from their serial numbers, later used to enter the United States, sometimes on multiple occasions. In some instances, entry was permitted even after the stolen passport had been posted in the lookout system.[3]

On the basis of this information, I asked that my Office of Inspections, Evaluations, and Special Review begin a review into this information. I do not comment on ongoing work, but I can advise you that the review has obtained additional documentation that, while still subject to further analysis, strongly suggests that stolen passports can be used successfully to enter the United States today. I will report to you on the further results of this review as soon as I am able.

I look forward now to the opportunity to answer your questions.

Chairman HYDE. Mr. Sullivan. Is it more convenient to go with Mr. Moss?

Mr. MOSS. Let me go, Mr. Chairman, because my testimony feeds into Mr. Sullivan's.

Chairman HYDE. Very well.

## STATEMENT OF FRANK MOSS, DEPUTY ASSISTANT SECRETARY FOR PASSPORT SERVICES, BUREAU OF CONSULAR AFFAIRS, U.S. DEPARTMENT OF STATE

Mr. MOSS. Mr. Chairman, Mr. Lantos, and Members of the Committee, it is a privilege to appear before you today to discuss the Department of State's efforts to strengthen the security of the U.S. passport and similar documents issued by other governments and to help prevent the travel of terrorists, organized crime members and others who wish to do us harm.

The State Department and many other governments are taking common action to help prevent passport misuse. The first objective is to ensure that passports are issued only to persons who are legitimately entitled to them. This is particularly important since physical improvements to passports such as photodigitized images of the bearer make it increasingly difficult to defeat internal security features.

To strengthen the adjudication process that determines whether someone is eligible for a U.S. passport, for example, the Department of State has recently signed a memorandum of understanding with the Social Security Administration. This will give us access to SSA data as a key element to help identify fraudulent applicants. We are also examining the role of commercial databases to identify cases of identity theft or other applications that require additional scrutiny.

[3] The passports of some countries contain two numbers: an inventory control number for the blank document and an issuance number added to the finished passport along with the bearer's personal information. In most instances, only the issuance number is queried against lookout lists, although it is the inventory control number that would have been entered into our lookout system had it been reported stolen by the foreign government.

Another key element is strengthening port of entry, POE, inspection. The international community, based on leadership by the United States and strong legislation enacted by the Congress, is hard at work introducing biometrics for use in a verification mode to help meet this goal. The member states of the International Civil Aviation Organization,ICAO, have approved the following globally interoperable biometrics specifications:

The baseline biometric will be facial recognition. Nations have the option of adding fingerprints and/or iris scans, but these biometrics may be for national government use and not necessarily globally interoperable.

The data will be written in the passport to an integrated circuit.

The data will include both the full facial image of the traveler as well as certain biographic data.

We have established international data transmission protocols consistent with International Standards Organization arrangements.

And, finally, we will use digital signature technology to ensure the security of the data.

U.S. plans, I should add, to introduce biometrics into U.S. passports are well advanced. Working in conjunction with the Government Printing Office, we have released to the industry our request for proposal to procure integrated circuits and the associated antenna arrays. We expect to award that contract later this year. We will be in limited production of biometric U.S. passports by the end of December, and we will start producing tourist passports next February.

In March 2005, there will be a multination test involving our colleagues from the Department of Homeland Security and other governments that are producing biometric passports by that date. We expect to complete the migration of the United States passport to an embedded one with embedded biometrics by the end of 2005.

Other governments have similar plans. Australia is close to production now. The European Union will begin producing passports with embedded biometrics as a new security feature by the end of 2005, and we expect Japan to have completed its transition by the first half of 2006.

Having a better passport, a strengthened adjudication system, and embedded biometrics will help prevent the misuse of passports. Another important step is sharing data electronically on lost and stolen passports. The State Department deployed our own Consular Lost and Stolen Passports—CLASP—database in 2002. This system provides lost and stolen U.S. passport data to all U.S. ports of entry within minutes of receiving this information. We have now expanded this critical program to the international level, as will be described in Mr. Sullivan's testimony.

The State Department recognizes that American citizens could be detained abroad based on information in the Interpol database. While this could be a case of data entry error on our part, a second scenario is that a citizen may report a passport as lost or stolen, subsequently locate the passport and then use it for travel. The State Department has recently issued regulations to establish that if a passport is reported as lost or stolen it is no longer valid for travel.

We have also established, in cooperation with the U.S. National Central Bureau and our consular colleagues here and abroad, standard procedures that will be used to help resolve quickly whether someone traveling on a passport is the authorized bearer.

We are confident that sharing U.S. data with Interpol will jump-start a broad-based international effort to share information on lost and stolen passports. To help make that happen, we are also encouraging the sharing of data through bilateral approaches to other governments and in international meetings such as the G–8 and at ICAO.

We are also looking at avenues beyond Interpol to exchange limited passport data. We have one bilateral effort under way with Australia. There is also early work being done on a multilateral initiative called Enhanced International Travel Security, or EITS. Both of these initiatives will take our efforts to a level where checks will be automatic and in real time.

A final initiative is an internal one. The Department of State will soon make available to DHS electronic images of all U.S. passport applications received since 1994. These images will help our border inspectors resolve questions about U.S. citizens, about persons returning to the United States and claiming to be U.S. citizens should such questions arise.

The State Department deeply appreciates the Committee's support for our strategy to improve the security of the U.S. passport and those issued by other governments. I look forward to your questions. Thank you very much.

Chairman HYDE. Thank you, Mr. Moss.

[The prepared statement of Mr. Moss follows:]

PREPARED STATEMENT OF FRANK MOSS, DEPUTY ASSISTANT SECRETARY FOR PASSPORT SERVICES, BUREAU OF CONSULAR AFFAIRS, U.S. DEPARTMENT OF STATE

Mr. Chairman and Members of the Committee:

I am Frank Moss, the Deputy Assistant Secretary for Passport Services at the Department of State, and it is a privilege to appear before you this morning regarding the efforts of the Department of State to prevent the use of lost or stolen passports by terrorists, criminals, and others who wish to do us harm.

The State Department, and our partners in the U.S. Visa Waiver Program, are taking a number of common steps to help prevent the misuse of passports. The first objective of the United States and governments throughout the world is to ensure that passports are issued only to persons who are legitimately entitled to them. This is particularly important since physical security improvements to passports—such as the use of photodigitized images of bearer—make it increasingly difficult to defeat the internal security features of a passport.

In the United States, we have a sophisticated passport application and adjudication process to help ensure that the person to whom we issue a passport is both a U.S. citizen and the person who the applicant claims to be. We are also actively exploring new initiatives in this area. We have recently signed a Memorandum of Understanding with the Social Security Administration so that the Department of State can use that agency's data as another element in our effort to identify fraudulent applicants. We are also examining the role of commercial databases to identify cases of identity theft or other applications that require additional scrutiny.

Another key element in improving the security of the international passport process is to strengthen the process used at ports-of-entry (POE) to ensure that the person traveling on a passport is the person to whom the passport was legitimately issued by his or her national government. The international community, based on leadership by the United States and strong legislation enacted by the Congress, has made great strides towards introducing biometrics that will be used in a "one-to-one verification" of the passport bearer to help meet this goal. Consistent with specifications established through the International Civil Aviation Organization, the United States and many other governments, particularly those that are the source of large numbers of temporary visitors to the United States, have launched comprehensive efforts to introduce biometrics into passports. The ICAO specifications, which were revised and received their final approval last month at a meeting in Montreal, call for a "globally interoperable" biometric system based on the following:

- The baseline biometric will be facial recognition. Nations have the option of adding to that fingerprints and/or iris scans, but these biometrics may be for national government use and thus not "globally interoperable;"
- The data will be written to an integrated circuit with a minimum storage capacity of 32 kb;
- The data will include the full facial image of the authorized bearer of the passport as well as other biographic data found on the data page of the passport;
- Data transmission standards will be consistent with protocols approved by the International Standards Organization; and,
- Digital signature technology will be used to secure data written to the integrated circuit.

As a point of reference, here is the status of U.S. plans to introduce biometrics into U.S. passports. Working in conjunction with our partners at the Government Printing Office, we currently have a Request for Proposal out to the industry. We expect to award a contract for the purchase of integrated circuits and the associated antenna array later this summer. We expect to produce our first operational passports this December at the Special Issuance Facility here in Washington. We will use government travelers as our test population in order to minimize problems for the general public should there be any production problems. We plan to begin producing tourist passports in February 2005 at our passport agency in Los Angeles. These books will then be used as part of a multi-nation interoperability test that will be undertaken by our colleagues from the Department of Homeland Security and their counterparts from other governments such as Australia and New Zealand that will by then also produce passports with embedded biometrics. Our current plan is to complete the migration to passports with embedded biometrics for all U.S. domestic passport production by the end of 2005.

Other governments that are the source of large numbers of visitors to the U.S. are working on a similar schedule. The European Union plans to begin introducing biometric passports by the end of 2005. Japan should complete its transition to embedded biometrics in early 2006. Many other governments should meet this objective around the same time.

Having a more secure passport, a strengthened adjudication system and embedded biometrics will help prevent the misuse of passports. Another important step in this process is sharing data electronically on lost and stolen passports. This has been a long-term goal of the Department of State and a key element in our efforts to frustrate the international travel of terrorists, criminals and alien smugglers. We developed and deployed our Consular Lost and Stolen Passports (CLASP) database in 2002. This initiative provides lost and stolen US passport data to all POEs within seconds of receiving the information. We have now expanded this critical program to the international level with the transfer in early May through our colleagues at the US National Central Bureau of limited data on over 300,000 lost or stolen U.S. passports to Interpol.

I know that there are questions about exactly what we have provided INTERPOL and how that data will be used. First, in terms of what has gone to INTERPOL it is only the passport number of the over 300,000 U.S. passports that have been reported as lost or stolen since April 2002 when we established our centralized database for this information. In addition, we have provided INTERPOL data to show that the lost document is a passport issued by the U.S. government. Second, this system as it currently operates, requires that a customs or immigration inspector become concerned about a traveler, then check with the U.S INTERPOL National Bureau and verify whether the passport has been reported as lost or stolen. Should that be the case, there would then be a concerted effort involving INTERPOL and the Departments of Justice and State to help determine whether the user of the passport is its authorized bearer.

There are at least two ways that a legitimate passport number could be found in the INTERPOL database. The first is nothing more than a data-entry error. No matter how hard we attempt to check our data before we turn it over to INTERPOL, it is almost inevitable that we will encounter an occasional data entry error. The second issue that we can foresee is that some people may report a passport as "lost or stolen," locate the passport , and then try to travel on that passport. The State Department has recently issued new regulations to make it clear that once a passport is reported as being lost or stolen it is no longer a valid travel document, but we are concerned that some people will still attempt to travel on such a passport. We have established in cooperation with the NCB and consular personnel in the Department of State standard procedures that we will apply to help resolve quickly and accurately whether someone seeking to use a U.S. passport for travel is in fact the authorized bearer of that document.

Our delivery of data on over 300,000 lost or stolen U.S. passports is an important step, but it is not the end of this process. We will update the data on a daily basis. More importantly, we have initiatives underway with INTERPOL that we hope will strengthen further the effectiveness of the INTERPOL database. A prime objective is to change the system so that it becomes a "business to business" process so that once a passport's machine readable zone is swiped, that is the two lines of data found at the bottom of the data page of a passport, data on lost and stolen passports, regardless of nation of issuance, can be made immediately available to immigration and custom officials of member states worldwide. This should help ensure that persons traveling on documents that may be lost or stolen are identified at primary inspection. Ann Barrett the Managing Director of Passport Services has recently traveled to INTERPOL headquarters to launch this effort. We know that it will take time for INTERPOL's systems to evolve to the point that data exchange is a totally electronic and near-real time process, but that remains our objective and that is shared by INTERPOL's senior management.

Another important effort that we have underway is to encourage other governments to join us in sharing data on lost or stolen passports with INTERPOL. We believe that the U.S. decision to share its data will help jumpstart a broad-based international effort. To help make that happen, we are also encouraging the sharing of such data through bilateral approaches to other governments and in international *fora* such as the G–8 and the International Civil Aviation Organization (ICAO). The U.S. has also taken steps to obtain comprehensive information from other countries on lost and stolen passports in the interim. As part of the Visa Waiver Program Country Review process, we have requested complete information on all lost and stolen blank passports from all VWP countries under review for the last 10 years. This information will be checked against information currently in the lookout system and added if necessary. We are also going to continue to closely monitor the lost and stolen blank passport situation to ensure complete and timely reporting by these countries.

The Department of State is also looking at other avenues beyond INTERPOL to facilitate the exchange of limited passport data in a real-time environment. Both of these initiatives would involve automated checks from ports of entry back to the country of passport issuance. One bilateral effort is underway with Australia and there is also early work underway on a multilateral initiative that includes ICAO, the Organization for Economic Cooperation and Development (OECD), and other potential groups called Enhanced International Travel Security or EITS. Both of these initiatives would take our efforts to ensure that passports borne by international travelers are legitimate documents to a new level where checks would be automatic and in real-time. Much work is needed to bring these initiatives to closure, but they offer alternative means to reaching our goal of preventing travel by international terrorists, criminals or other persons of concern on lost of stolen passports.

A final initiative that we have underway is strictly a U.S. initiative. It involves making available to Customs and Border Protection Officers at POEs an electronic image of all passport applications received since 1994 to assist in resolving questions about the *bona fides* of persons claiming to be American citizens. The United States is encouraging the development and promotion of the initiatives mentioned in a manner that is informed by privacy policy guidance on maximizing individual privacy protections and information security.

The State Department appreciates the encouragement that we have received from this Committee and others as we have pursued our strategy to improve the security of the U.S. passport and those issued by other governments. We are especially appreciative of your support for our efforts to share internationally data on lost or stolen U.S. passports. I would be pleased to answer your questions about our overall strategy to help make U.S. and foreign borders more secure through improvements to the entire passport process. Thank you.

Chairman HYDE. And now, Mr. Sullivan.

**STATEMENT OF JAMES M. SULLIVAN, DIRECTOR, U.S. NATIONAL CENTRAL BUREAU, INTERPOL CRIMINAL POLICE ORGANIZATION, U.S. DEPARTMENT OF JUSTICE**

Mr. SULLIVAN. Thank you, Mr. Chairman, Congressman Lantos. On behalf of U.S. National Central Bureau of Interpol I thank you for the opportunity to brief on Interpol's activities in the area of lost and stolen travel documents.

While significant efforts have been made to better control the issuance of passports, these documents continue to be vulnerable to illegitimate use. Despite the best security efforts, every nation has experienced losses and thefts of its travel documents. Furthermore, organized crime figures target certain countries because of the value of their documents and the ease of travel that they afford.

In one case, a subject used a stolen Greek passport to enter Bulgaria and legally sponsored 10 immigrants into the country. In another example, a Serbian suspect used a stolen Croatian passport to travel extensively throughout Europe. The subject was ultimately charged with involvement in the murder of the Serbian Prime Minister.

It is difficult for Interpol to determine the extent to which terrorist organizations are involved. All countries are vulnerable. This vulnerability can best be addressed if global law enforcement share passport and identification document information. Interpol can perform this function.

Interpol's Automated Search Facility/Stolen Travel Document Database, or ASF/STB, became operational in July 2002. It is a screening tool for law enforcement and border protection entities. The information it provides thwarts the illegal travel of international terrorists and criminals. The Interpol database presently contains approximately 1.6 million records actively reported by 41 Interpol member countries.

As you have heard, in May 2004, the Department of State Bureau of Consular Affairs announced U.S. participation in the Interpol program through the transfer of over 300,000 passport records.

The G–8 has also endorsed the Interpol ASF/STD system; and earlier this month the G–8 heads of state formally announced their participation in the program through the sharing of national data on lost and stolen passports, both issued and blank, by December 2004. This support recognizes the role of Interpol as the world's only truly global law enforcement network. It further legitimizes the program and encourages increased participation by our foreign counterparts.

Of the 1.6 million records, approximately 60 percent are passports predominantly lost or stolen from the bearer, while 40 percent are national identification documents.

Through Interpol's I–24/7 telecommunication system, law enforcement officials in the 181 Interpol member countries can query the database to obtain information about the country of issuance, the date of theft or loss, and other related information as provided by the reporting country.

I would like to stress that Interpol does not—and I repeat not—store any personal information relating to the legitimate bearer of the passport. This ensures the sharing of information without violating the privacy of U.S. citizens. Moreover, Interpol's I–24/7 communications system provides excellent protection for the data through its secure, encrypted, internet-based browser technology. This system also allows placement of restrictions on who can access the system. Accordingly, we have taken action that prevents restricted countries such as Cuba, Iran, Libya, Sudan and Syria from accessing U.S. information.

USNCB–Interpol Washington coordinates U.S. participation in the program and will be responsible for the regular transfer and updating of U.S. data to the base. The USNCB will automatically be notified each time a law enforcement authority searches the database and receives a hit. We will immediately go about the standard procedure of hit confirmation and follow up with our foreign counterparts to coordinate the appropriate law enforcement response.

As pointed out by Mr. Moss, the manner in which the system currently operates is quite passive. An immigration or border official must suspect the authenticity of a traveler's documentation and in each case query the Interpol system. Obviously, requiring border officials to perform this extra query is not the most effective means of checking the enormous volume of travelers who cross our borders. This is why Interpol recognizes the need to establish a systematic and routine mechanism for widespread use of the database at border points.

The ultimate objective is a business-to-business arrangement, commonly referred to as B2B, whereby national data can be queried through Interpol channels automatically with the swipe of every passport at every port of entry through use of the passport's machine readable zone. This mechanism is the only way to ensure the ultimate success of this program on a global scale. One advantage for the United States would be that the data will reside locally and we will be in a better position to control and monitor access to our information.

The B2B concept is an ambitious but necessary achievable goal, provided that the proper resources are dedicated to the program. In early June, U.S. and European Union officials met in Lyon on this matter. At that time, Interpol committed itself to implementing a B2B proof of concept among a small group of countries within the next 3 months. This endeavor is not without cost for the Interpol General Secretariat and illustrates the importance that Secretary General Ronald Noble has placed on this program.

To date, no Interpol country is routinely querying the database at its ports of entry. The United States has conducted limited queries of the Interpol database. This is due to lack of awareness about the system by U.S. law enforcement. In order to rectify the situation, USNCB recently alerted Federal, State and local law enforcement to the existence of this Interpol tool.

The broadcast communication informed U.S. law enforcement of the procedures in place for querying foreign and domestic passport numbers and the assistance provided through the United States National Central Bureau and the Department of State. We are also working closely with the Department of Homeland Security National Targeting Center to provide it with direct query access in the short term. This will enable the National Targeting Center to query advanced passenger information against Interpol's database. Ultimately, however, the B2B approach is the only way we will achieve broad, systematic use of the system at U.S. ports of entry. This will require significant technical collaboration between the United States National Central Bureau and the Department of Homeland Security.

This program is in its infancy. It is the first step toward a systemic global law enforcement approach to thwart the illegal use of travel documents. Its success will depend on the ability of each Interpol member country to respond to queries on a 24-hour basis and the establishment of globally accepted best practices or standard operating procedures for the handling of hit information. With the support of countries like the United States, Interpol can be a leader in this effort.

I would like to thank you for your time and interest in what we believe is a very important Interpol tool. I will be happy to address any questions you may have.

Chairman HYDE. Thank you, Mr. Sullivan.

[The prepared statement of Mr. Sullivan follows:]

PREPARED STATEMENT OF JAMES M. SULLIVAN, DIRECTOR, U.S. NATIONAL CENTRAL BUREAU, INTERPOL CRIMINAL POLICE ORGANIZATION, U.S. DEPARTMENT OF JUSTICE

Mr. Chairman and Members of the Committee:

On behalf of the U.S. National Central Bureau, INTERPOL, a component of the Department of Justice, I thank you for the opportunity to brief on Interpol's activities in the area of lost and stolen travel documents.

The events of September 2001 prompted a serious review, at an international level, of controls on the issuance, handling and delivery of official travel documents. While significant efforts have been made to centralize and better control passport issuance procedures, such documents continue to be vulnerable to illegitimate use by the world's criminal element. Despite best security efforts, nearly every nation has experienced losses and thefts of its travel documents. Furthermore, organized crime figures target certain countries because of the value of their documents and the ease of travel that they afford. In one case, a subject used a stolen Greek passport to enter Bulgaria and legally sponsored 10 immigrants into the country. In another example, a Serbian subject used a stolen Croatian passport to travel extensively throughout Europe. The subject was ultimately charged with involvement in the murder of the Serbian Prime Minister.

At a national level, the airline hijackings of September 11th spurred a reevaluation of the penalties surrounding the use of passports and other false documents for illegal entry into the United States. In response to these security concerns, the Department of Justice and the Department of State approached the United States Sentencing Commission in its last amendment cycle, requesting penalty increases for defendants who fraudulently use or obtain United States passports or other false documents. The Commission took the first step by voting to promulgate amendments addressing some of these offenses, increasing penalties by approximately 50 percent for defendants who fraudulently obtain or use a United States passport, and approving upward departures for defendants who fraudulently obtain or use a passport with the intent to engage in terrorist activity. Furthermore, the Commission has expressed a commitment to complete its revision of the issue in the upcoming amendment cycle.

While there are countless examples of the use of illegally obtained passports, it is difficult for INTERPOL to determine the extent of terrorist organizations involvement, direct or indirect. Suffice to say, a fraudulently obtained passport provides criminals and terrorists alike with the opportunity to travel virtually unidentified, and we must assume that they will make every attempt to exploit that opportunity. Unfortunately, all countries are vulnerable to this risk and we simply cannot afford *not* to share information on stolen or lost travel documents with our foreign law enforcement counterparts. INTERPOL can perform this mission.

INTERPOL's Automated Search Facility/Stolen Travel Document Database (ASF–STD) became operational in July 2002, after four years of development. The ASF/STD is a screening tool for law enforcement and border protection entities. It serves to provide information about lost or stolen documents to the international law enforcement community, thereby thwarting the illicit travel of international terrorists and criminals.

Specifically, the ASF/STD contains the identification numbers of lost or stolen national identity and travel documents, such as stolen passports and visas, *and* national administrative documents, such as vehicle registrations. Through INTERPOL's 'I–24/7' telecommunications system, law enforcement officials in the 181–INTERPOL member countries, can query the database and obtain information about invalidated documents, their country of issuance, date of theft or loss, and other related information as provided by the reporting country.

The INTERPOL database presently contains approximately 1.6 million records, reported by forty-one different participating member countries[1]. These include three G8 nations, several of the U.S. visa waiver countries, and countries in all four of INTERPOL's geographical regions: Asia, Africa, Europe and the Americas. I have provided, for the record, the mandatory and optional data fields contained in the system. Countries such as Canada, Japan, and the United Kingdom have committed themselves to supplying data by the end of this year. Of the 1.6 million records, approximately 60% are passports, predominately lost or stolen from bearer, while 40% are national identification documents.

The INTERPOL program is in its infancy and its global success will depend largely on the leadership of countries like the United States. As you have heard, in May 2004, the Department of State, Bureau of Consular Affairs, announced U.S. participation in the INTERPOL program through the transfer of over 300,000 records of U.S. lost and stolen passports to the database. This announcement was the result of months of inter-agency coordination among the U.S. government and law enforcement entities responsible for passport issuance and border protection. This act was the first step in preventing lost and stolen U.S. passports from criminal use.

The G8 has also endorsed the INTERPOL ASF/STD system, and earlier this month, the G8 Heads of State formally announced their participation in the program through the sharing of national data on lost and stolen passports (issued and blank), by December 2004. This support recognizes the role of INTERPOL as the world's *only* truly global law enforcement network. It will further legitimize the program and encourage increased participation by foreign counterparts.

USNCBBINTERPOL Washington coordinates U.S. participation in this program and will be responsible for ensuring the regular transfer and updating of U.S. lost/stolen passport data to the INTERPOL database. The USNCB also serves as the primary point of contact for all "hits" to U.S. passport data and coordination with foreign law enforcement counterparts through INTERPOL's communications network. "Hits" on U.S. lost/stolen data will be handled in consultation with the appropriate U.S. authorities to confirm the bona fides of the individual presenting the document, identify any criminal antecedents, and coordinate subsequent law enforcement action, as necessary.

I would like to stress that INTERPOL does not store any personal information relating to the legitimate bearer of the passport. This enables the sharing of lost/stolen information, without violating the privacy of a U.S. citizen, who may be the victim of a theft or simply lost a passport that subsequently fell into the hands of a criminal. Moreover, INTERPOL's I–24/7 communications system provides excellent protection for the data: it is a secure, virtual private network utilizing encrypted servers (3–DES) and internet-based browser technology. The system also provides the capability of placing restrictions on who can access information. Thus, in accordance with U.S. policy, we have taken action that prevents restricted countries (*i.e.*, Cuba, Iran, Libya, Sudan, and Syria) from accessing U.S. lost and stolen passport data.

How will we know who is checking our data? Each time a foreign law enforcement authority searches the database and receives a "hit" on a known lost or stolen U.S. passport, USNCB will be automatically notified. Immediately, we will go about the standard procedure of "hit" confirmation and follow-up with foreign counterparts to coordinate the appropriate law enforcement response. Thanks to our close collaboration with the Department of State, and in particular, Mr. Moss' office, we are generally able to respond to such inquiries in a matter of minutes. USNCB–INTERPOL Washington will also continue to coordinate its efforts with components of the DHS

[1] As of 10 June 2004, the following countries were participants in the ASF/STD program: Armenia, Australia, Bahamas, Belarus, Belgium, Bosnia Herzegovina, Brazil, Burundi, Colombia, Croatia, Cyprus, Estonia, France, FYROM, Gabon, Greece, Hong Kong, Italy, Jordan, Kenya, Kirgizia, Kuwait, Lebanon, Lithuania, Luxembourg, Malta, Niger, Pakistan, Portugal, Qatar, Saudi Arabia, Senegal, Seychelles, Slovenia, South Africa, Syria, Ukraine, Uruguay, USA, Zimbabwe.

to ensure that INTERPOL information can be accessed by various customs and border protection entities in a timely and secure manner.

To date, no INTERPOL country is routinely querying this database at its ports of entry. Nevertheless, queries of the database more than doubled in the first quarter of 2004. We therefore anticipate that foreign and domestic counterparts who wish to access this data will increasingly solicit the USNCB.

As pointed out by Mr. Moss' testimony, the manner in which this system currently operates is quite passive. An immigration or border official must suspect the authenticity of a traveler's documentation and in each case query the INTERPOL system. Obviously, requiring border officials to perform this extra query is not the most effective means of checking the enormous volume of travelers crossing our borders on a daily basis. This is why INTERPOL recognizes the need to establish a systematic and routine mechanism for widespread use of the database at border points. The ultimate objective is a "business-to-business" arrangement (commonly called "B2B"), whereby national data can be queried through INTERPOL channels automatically with the swipe of *every* passport at *every* point of entry, through use of the passport's machine readable zone. This mechanism is the only way to ensure the ultimate success of this program on a global scale. One advantage for the United States would be that data will reside locally, and we will be in a better position to control and monitor access to our information.

The B2B concept is an ambitious but necessary and achievable goal, provided that the proper resources are dedicated to the program. In early June, U.S. and EU officials met in Lyon on this matter. At that time, INTERPOL committed itself to implementing a "B2B proof of concept" among a small group of countries within the next three months. This endeavor is not without significant costs for the INTERPOL General Secretariat and illustrates the importance that Secretary General Ronald Noble has placed on this program.

To date, the United States has conducted limited queries of the INTERPOL database. This is due, in part, to a lack of awareness about the system on the part of U.S. law enforcement. In order to rectify this situation, the USNCB recently alerted federal, state and local law enforcement to the existence of this INTERPOL tool. The broadcast communication informed U.S. law enforcement of the procedures in place for querying foreign and domestic passport numbers, and the assistance provided through the USNCB and the Department of State. We are also working closely with DHS' National Targeting Center (NTC) to provide it with direct query access in the short-term. This will enable NTC to query advanced passenger information against INTERPOL databases. Ultimately, however, the B2B approach is the only way that we will achieve broad, systematic use of the system at U.S. ports of entry. This will require significant technical collaboration between the USNCB and DHS.

While this program is in its infancy, we feel that it is the first step towards a systematic, global law enforcement approach to thwart the illegal use of travel documents. Its success will, of course, depend on the ability of each INTERPOL member country to respond to inquiries on a 24-hour basis, and the establishment of globally accepted "best practices" (e.g., standard operating procedures) for the handling of 'hit' information. With the support of countries like the United States, INTERPOL can be a leader in this effort.

Thank you for your time and interest in what we believe is a very important INTERPOL tool. I would be happy to address any questions you may have.

## *Populating ASF/STD: Required Fields*

- ✓ **Issuing Country of document**
- ✓ **Document Type**
- ✓ **Document Identity Number**
- ✓ **Country of Theft/Loss**
- ✓ **Type of Fraud (STB or STL)**

## *Populating ASF/STD: Optional Fields*

- ❑ **National Reference Number**
- ❑ **Date of Theft**
- ❑ **Place of Theft**
- ❑ **Additional Information (free text)**
- ❑ **Print Batch Number (free text)**

Chairman HYDE. We will now entertain questions; and, first, Mr. Lantos.

Mr. LANTOS. Thank you very much, Mr. Chairman.

I want to thank all three of our distinguished witnesses for their very illuminating testimony.

Let me walk you through my understanding of the issue we are dealing with. I take it that if a person comes from a country where we require a visa, we have some standard of security, because the applicant has to appear at a U.S. Embassy or Consular Office and demonstrate that he is qualified to obtain a visa. But we have a very large number of countries where the visa is not required. Am I correct in this?

Mr. ERVIN. Yes, sir.

Mr. LANTOS. Now one of these countries happens to be France, is that correct? If I am a French citizen or I come from France, I do not require a visa, is that correct?

Mr. ERVIN. That is right, sir.

Mr. LANTOS. My understanding is there has been an enormous theft of blank French passports in recent times, running into the thousands.

Mr. ERVIN. That is our understanding as well.

Mr. LANTOS. How do we deal with this issue? What is the training of our immigration officers at the points of entry? What do we do if you present a stolen French passport, fraudulent French passport? And my understanding is, by the way, that even if our immigration officer discovers that the document is false, it is a fraud, he returns it to the individual so he can return to his country of origin, rather than having him arrested and having him deported. Enlighten me on this, please.

Mr. ERVIN. Yes, sir. Two issues there. With regard to the training of the port of entry inspectors, it pales in comparison to the training that is provided to consular officers overseas before whom visa applicants must appear, as you suggested.

With regard to the training of the inspectors, they have only 1 day out of 1 week of training, new inspectors, only 1 day of training that is devoted to the detection of fraud. Most of the training that does occur is conducted at the local level. As we understand it, there has been inadequate funding for experienced teams of inspectors to go from place to place locally to give the benefit of their expertise to new or relatively new inspectors. So training needs to be beefed up significantly.

With regard to the issue of the return of a passport that is discovered to be fraudulent, that is indeed the case. We have recommended to the Border and Transportation Security Directorate that they review that process. They have agreed to do so.

There is a provision in ICAO that appears to permit, at least under certain circumstances, the travel document to be returned annotated with some suggestion that the document is fraudulent. Then the traveler could be given some travel papers and then that person would be sent back to his or her country of origin, but at least there would be some indication that that person attempted to enter our country with a fraudulent document. But, as I say, that needs to be reviewed. We understand that BTS is reviewing it; and it is troubling, as you suggest.

Mr. LANTOS. Do either of the two other gentlemen want to comment on my question?

Mr. MOSS. Mr. Lantos, I would like to provide a little additional background information on the French loss of their of passports.

What happens in a case like that is they have notified the U.S. Embassy in Paris. They have immediately notified our own fraud prevention people at the Department of State. We immediately enter the numbers of the stolen passports into the databases, including the—I believe it is called the Treasury Enforcement Customs Systems, TECS database, which then flows through to DHS for use by the inspectors at ports of entry.

We found out about the most recent French loss within a matter of hours after it happened. Clearly, the French losses are a matter of concern to us. We are also, I might add, working with all of our Visa Waiver Program countries to educate the countries on the importance of giving us information on both lost blanks as well as lost personalized passports. We have sent out messages about that as recently as a month ago. And, clearly, the process is under way right now between State and DHS to review the continued eligibility of countries for the Visa Waiver Program, is looking at this program as well. Thank you.

Mr. LANTOS. Mr. Sullivan.

Mr. SULLIVAN. Thank you, Congressman.

First of all, France is one of the members of the 41-member countries that provides information to this database; and my understanding is all of those numbers are currently in the Interpol database.

The process that we have—and it has been ongoing for several years—is we have a State Department agent from the Department of Diplomatic Security who is assigned at the United States National Central Bureau. When they receive information on stolen passports, the document is forwarded to the Stolen Passports Group. The Stolen Passports Group consists of six components. They are the Analysis and Infrastructure Protection Unit at DHS; the Foreign Terrorism Task Force at the FBI; the Forensic Document Lab at ICE; the Intelligence Division at ICE; the National Targeting Center, who I spoke about before; and the Visa and Fraud Prevention at the Department of State.

I think this indicates, as Mr. Moss has said, that it is better to receive the information from many sources to make sure none of the information slips through and that when the information is received that we share it with as many people as possible so that we know when the databases are checked we have the best information possible for law enforcement who is looking to find out the validity of these travel documents.

Thank you.

Mr. LANTOS. May I raise one more question, Mr. Chairman?

Chairman HYDE. Surely.

Mr. LANTOS. There was a study done by the Center for Immigration Studies. They compiled a list of 48 militant Islamic terrorists who have been charged, convicted, pled guilty or admitted to involvement in terrorism in the United States in the last decade; and these 48 violent Islamic terrorists entered the United States on the following basis: 23 had tourist visas, three had business visas, one applied for asylum, five had student visas, one had a seat in transit visa, one had a forged Swedish passport, one had a forged Canadian passport, and three of them entered without inspection.

Now this is a horrendous record. How much progress have we made? Because this clearly is the Achilles heel of our security system. I mean, we are—and I am not in the least critical—we are processing millions of people coming to this country with great speed at many points of entry, and the task is a gargantuan one, but could this list occur today that I just read to you, Mr. Ervin?

Mr. ERVIN. Yes, Congressman, it could.

Mr. LANTOS. Well, that means we are like a sieve. There is really no effective way we are keeping these people out.

Mr. ERVIN. Well, there are problems. There are vulnerabilities. That was the subject of our report. As you heard and as we noted, efforts are underway on the part of the State Department, on the part of the Department of Homeland Security, on the part of Interpol and other partners to address all of these issues; and we applaud that. But more needs to be done more quickly because, as you suggest, these are security vulnerabilities to which strict attention should be paid.

Mr. LANTOS. If I may conclude with this, which of the countries which do not have visa requirements create most of our problems? I would like to ask you to name names because diplomatic niceties are irrelevant when we talk about potential terrorism.

Mr. MOSS. Mr. Lantos, what I would say, it is not necessarily specific countries that create problems. It is often systems within those countries

Mr. LANTOS. Well, in which countries are there systems which create problems for us?

Mr. MOSS. I think, sir, what I would say, it is countries that have highly decentralized passport production systems. I am talking about countries where passports are made at the equivalent of the city hall, for example. Therefore, you have passports, blank books being stored in dozens or perhaps hundreds of locations.

Mr. LANTOS. What countries are these, Mr. Moss? Name the countries.

Mr. MOSS. Well, certainly in the past Belgium has had such a system. They have now gone to a new system of centralized production.

The French have had a similar system of decentralized production, as you have noted in our own information on theft. I will be happy to provide you for the record information on whether the French are examining their decentralized system in light of the record that you reported earlier about thefts of French passports. I would like to provide that for the record, however.

Mr. LANTOS. As far as you know, the French still have a decentralized system of issuing passports.

Mr. MOSS. Sir, I would like to confirm that with our Embassy in Paris and the French authorities and provide that for the record, if I may.

Mr. LANTOS. Are there any other countries which have a decentralized system of issuing passports?

Mr. MOSS. Many countries, sir, because of new technology—and I mention in my testimony, for example, photodigitization—have actually gone to centralized production systems. Many other countries as well, because of vulnerabilities with passports issued by Embassies and consulates abroad, have actually repatriated that work back to their home country or maybe two or three locations around the world.

There certainly, sir, is a shared recognition by countries all over the world, in the Visa Waiver Program and outside of it, of the need to strengthen the entire passport process so that bad books are, first of all, not issued inadvertently and that books that are stolen or lost can be identified or tracked through systems like Interpol. There really is a new thinking on this process and one that certainly your legislation has encouraged and I think certainly the work of the State Department and our colleagues at DHS encourages on a daily basis in capitals around the world.

Mr. LANTOS. What criteria does a country have to meet to move into the category of not requiring visas?

Mr. ERVIN. Well, traditionally, sir, the basis for the visa waiver country entrance has been a historically low rate of overstay of the visa, a historically low rate of the refusal of visa issuance to that country. That is the historical basis for it. Because, historically, the concern was that visas not be given to those who actually intended to be immigrants, as opposed to mere visitors.

Mr. LANTOS. But the emphasis has now shifted to preventing terrorism.

Mr. ERVIN. That is right. That is right.

Mr. LANTOS. So if I am now a country that requires visas, how do I graduate to the other category?

Mr. ERVIN. If you are a country that requires visas?

Mr. LANTOS. At the moment.

Mr. ERVIN. Well, I do not know that there is a process in place now to graduate, as you put it. I should think just following the logic that if over time a country establishes that it has a good record with regard to the issues that we are talking about here that that would be a basis and perhaps the basis for that.

Mr. LANTOS. Thank you, Mr. Chairman.

Chairman HYDE. Thank you.

Mr. Pitts.

Mr. PITTS. Thank you, Mr. Chairman.

How many U.S. passports were reported stolen for the last, say, 3 years, for the year 2000 to today, blank and issued?

Mr. MOSS. First of all, Mr. Pitts, in the question of blank U.S. passports, the number is essentially zero. We have an credibly sophisticated system to ensure that U.S. passports do not go missing.

In terms of lost personalized passports, lost or stolen, we have approximately 320,000 recorded in our system, going back to 2002; and I should add that the number that we are seeing has probably increased because of outreach efforts to the public as well as steps we have taken abroad that we cannot replace a U.S. passport reported as lost or stolen without making entries into our CLASP database. So we have a much better idea of the current lost rate than we may have had about numbers 5 years ago. But I do want to assure you we have very sophisticated efforts in place to ensure that U.S. blank passports do not go missing.

Mr. PITTS. So how many U.S. passports were reported stolen last year?

Mr. MOSS. Sir, I could break that down for the record. All I can say right now is about 200,000 a year go into our database. I would like to check that as to the breakout between lost passports and ones that are reported as being stolen, if I may.

Mr. PITTS. In what databases are these passports found? National? International?

Mr. MOSS. Sir, they start with being in a U.S. database at the Department of State called the Consular Lost and Stolen Passports database. The information in that database then flows from there to DHS databases so information is available at ports of entry; and, as we discussed this morning, we are now sharing certain elements of that database through Interpol with governments all over the world. So it is shared on both the national level as well as internationally.

Mr. PITTS. How many stolen passports are believed to be in circulation today? Perhaps Mr. Sullivan. And where are most of them from?

Mr. SULLIVAN. Congressman, our best estimate for 55 countries, of the 181 countries of Interpol are in excess of 10 million. So I do not think we have a final figure, but they are in the millions of missing or stolen passports.

Mr. PITTS. What region of the world, what countries are most of them from?

Mr. SULLIVAN. That is a very difficult question to answer. They are from all over. Obviously, they are European. A lot are U.S. passports, there is 300,000 plus of those. I do not think I could give you specifically what countries. It is more based on who has international travel, what countries are doing international travel. I would say it is probably more European based than anything else because they have a tendency to travel internationally more than any other country.

Mr. PITTS. Under the Visa Waiver Program an individual can enter the U.S. for 90 days for tourism or business. A lot can be accomplished in 90 days by terrorists. Why is the number set at 90 days? Has there been any study done on limiting the amount of time that an individual can stay in the United States?

Mr. ERVIN. None that I am aware of, sir, but I defer to the Department of State on that.

Mr. MOSS. Congressman, I will check this for the record, but I believe, actually, that some of the requirements involving the Visa Waiver Program are actually set in law. I will check and see if the 90 days is a legislative matter or regulatory and get back to you, get back to the staff this afternoon if I could.

Mr. PITTS. Is there any information on how many times an individual can visit the U.S. under the Visa Waiver Program and how much time must elapse between a visit under the Visa Waiver Program and another visit? Is there any mechanism to track individuals who enter the U.S. on multiple occasions under the Visa Waiver Program?

Mr. MOSS. Let me take a crack at that, if I can.

The requirement is that the individual be in the United States for no more than 90 days. They must then leave.

There are people who make multiple trips. For example, this does facilitate the travel of international businessmen. They may not be staying for the 90 days. They may be staying 2 or 3 days, but they may travel 20 times during a given year.

On the second question about tracking the persons as they enter the United States, of course, we have our DHS systems, but they will then be augmented in September with the introduction of the expansion, I should say, of US–VISIT to cover Visa Waiver Program travelers. That will involve the entry of about 13 million additional persons through US–VISIT, and that will give us both better data as well as biometrics, in this case finger scans and photos, of those travelers as part of the US–VISIT system.

I will turn this over now to Mr. Ervin.

Mr. ERVIN. Let me underscore how important we believe in the Office of Inspector General that the application of US–VISIT to visa waiver travelers is. Because until that application is made—and as we understand it that will begin to be done in September—until that is the case, there really is no way of knowing exactly how many people are entering our country through the Visa Waiver Program, no organized way of knowing that, and no way of having an exit system. The US–VISIT is designed to be an entry and exit checkout system, as you know.

Chairman HYDE. The gentleman's time has expired.

Mrs. Davis.

Mrs. DAVIS. Why would we want to continue with the Visa Waiver Program when we have to worry about terrorists coming in? If I just heard you correctly, you can use the Visa Waiver Program and be here virtually the entire year, just go back for a day or 2, come back, back for a day or 2 and come back.

Mr. MOSS. Congresswoman, I think the Visa Waiver Program is an important element not just in our border inspection process and our consulate work overseas, but it is also important in encouraging business and tourism in the United States. It is also one that applies reciprocal benefits to American citizens as they travel abroad, and I think it is that totality of issues that led the Congress in the late 1980s and to subsequently reauthorize it since then, that the Visa Waiver Program is a legislative initiative. It is one that we believe is important to the global economy as well as to industries in the United States. We think that the benefits of the Visa Waiver Program are very significant.

Mrs. DAVIS. As long as that industry is not terrorism, I do not have a problem with it. Of the 10 million lost or stolen passports that you were talking about, are they mostly from countries that have the Visa Waiver Program or are they just scattered?

Mr. SULLIVAN. I would say they are scattered. I could not identify exactly whether they are from the visa waiver countries or not. It is a worldwide problem. It is not specific to any one country, including the United States. We have travelers who lose their passports or have them stolen all the time. So I do not think I can give you an answer to that question. I am sorry.

Mr. ERVIN. If I may, Congresswoman, we may be able to shed some light on at least an aspect of that issue when we complete the review we have under way. As you heard me say, we are in the process now, based upon this report, of doing another which will focus on the number of lost and stolen passports that are used to enter our country. So we will have some sense based on that review of the countries from which those passports come.

Mrs. DAVIS. Let me follow up on a question that Mr. Lantos had. It boggled my mind when I heard you confirm that, in fact, if we catch someone with a lost or stolen passport in their possession we give it back to them.

Mr. ERVIN. That is the practice.

Mrs. DAVIS. Is that practice going to be changed?

Mr. ERVIN. I hope so. We recommended that it be changed; and BTS, the applicable directorate in the Department, has agreed that that needs to be reviewed.

Mr. LANTOS. Will the gentlewoman yield?

Mrs. DAVIS. Yes.

Mr. LANTOS. When did you recommend that idiotic procedure be changed?

Mr. ERVIN. Our draft report was issued to the Department on March 11.

Mr. LANTOS. And they have agreed to take it under advisement?

Mr. ERVIN. Essentially so, that is right; and their comments were given to us on the 28th of May, I think it was.

Mr. LANTOS. And what were the reasons for not changing this moronic procedure?

Mr. ERVIN. At the risk of appearing to speak for them—and I certainly do not want to do that—they take the position that there is some ambiguity as to whether they, DHS, has the legal right to do anything other than to return the passport to the traveler.

Mr. LANTOS. So let me get it straight. I am a potential terrorist. I buy a stolen French passport. An eagle-eyed inspector detects that it is a stolen French passport. He then returns it to me so I may return to France on my stolen fraudulent passport so I can buy another fraudulent passport and try to enter the United States a week later. Is that the current procedure?

Mr. ERVIN. That is the current procedure.

Mr. LANTOS. An insane asylum would be embarrassed to have such a procedure; and I suggest, Mr. Chairman, that you and I perhaps write a letter to the Secretary concerning this.

Chairman HYDE. I certainly agree with your suggestion and the point you are making.

Mrs. Davis you still have some time.

Mr. LANTOS. Thank you for yielding, Mrs. Davis.

Mrs. DAVIS. You are welcome, Mr. Lantos.

I thank the Chairman.

Mr. ROHRABACHER. This has been a very interesting hearing, and I have been looking through some of my notes at some past hearings here. It was just a few weeks ago someone testified in your very same seat, Mr. Ervin, that when someone comes in now to this country, that we do have a record of when they come in and when they leave. I am trying to figure that out. Is that correct?

Mr. ERVIN. Well, what I was referring is the US–VISIT program. The US–VISIT program——

Mr. ROHRABACHER. I am talking about, right now, anyone who comes into this country, do we have also the record of when they return to their home country?

Mr. ERVIN. No, we do not. There is at present no exit system. There is no——

Mr. ROHRABACHER. If I might note for you, Mr. Chairman, that we had a hearing here just a few weeks ago in which a witness from this Administration said just the opposite of what I am hearing right now. Said that, yes, we have an exit identification program so that we know when people leave the country—and now we are being told that that is not true.

Mr. ERVIN. Right. Just to complete the sentence, the US–VISIT program is intended to be both an entry and exit system. It is in operation, as you know, at 115 airports and at 14 seaports. There is a test program, a pilot program that has an exit feature at one airport and at one seaport. But right now in place today there is no formal exit system at all of our ports of entry.

Mr. ROHRABACHER. If someone has a visa to come here, first of all—I will get to the visa waiver countries next. If someone has a visa to come here, we have issued this visa, and he or she is on the list of people that have that visa, then do we have a system that says, okay, this person came in and this person now has returned and we know they are back in their home country? Do we have that?

Mr. ERVIN. Yes. Well, we do not have an exit system. We know that that person has entered. There is no formal, regularized exit system is what I am saying. There is something called an I–94 form which one completes, and there is a part of that form that you are supposed to return when you depart. Sometimes it is returned. Sometimes it is not. Sometimes it is solicited on departure, and sometimes it is not. So there is no formal——

Mr. ROHRABACHER. So there is no type of situation——

Mr. ERVIN. There is no formal procedure.

Mr. ROHRABACHER. Mr. Chairman, just to note, this is exactly opposite from what was testified here just 2 or 3 weeks ago. I will find out exactly who that witness was. This is outrageous, because this is a very significant point.

Now in terms of the illegal immigration to this country, most illegal immigrants, are they not, are just people who have come in here and just overstayed their visa and just decided to forget how long the visa is for and they just stay here, is that correct?

Mr. ERVIN. Well, I would like to defer to my State Department colleagues on that. I do not think it is fair to say illegal immigrants are here because of visas, because many of them enter without having visas.

Mr. ROHRABACHER. Yes, but most. People talk about people coming here illegally. The fact is that most illegal immigrants, I believe from what I have seen, have come here with a visa.

Mr. MOSS. Mr. Rohrabacher, my understanding is that the overwhelming majority of illegal persons in the United States have entered without inspection. That means that they have come across our land borders. The figures that range on the number of overstays are imprecise, but the high number I have heard is perhaps 40 percent. I have heard more recently numbers that were perhaps in the low 20 percent. But, obviously, the difference are people—and, in any event, more than a majority are people who entered without inspection.

Mr. ROHRABACHER. Where did you get that figure?

Mr. MOSS. The enter without inspection figure, sir?

Mr. ROHRABACHER. Right.

Mr. MOSS. Sir, I will have to go back to my office and check, but these are figures that——

Mr. ROHRABACHER. I will have to tell you that I would like you to go back and get that, because I would like to know what is accurate on this. From other people, I have heard a far different assessment from that.

Mr. MOSS. Sir, I will have that to the Committee staff within a few hours.

Mr. ROHRABACHER. How many visas do we issue to mainland China every year?

Mr. MOSS. Sir, the number of visas issued in China is in the several hundred thousand a year range. I am sorry, I do not have that exact number with me. But, again, I can give you that. It is one of our largest visa-issuing operations in the world right now.

Mr. ROHRABACHER. Right. You have not noticed a significant difference in the illegal immigration in people from China in our country in the last couple of years?

Mr. MOSS. Sir, there is clearly a major problem with illegal migration from China. I do not think that most of that illegal migration though is via the visa route. There are literally organized rings charging 40, 50, even $60,000 to smuggle people around the world in order to enter people in the United States. I think that is a major source of the illegal migration from China.

Mr. ROHRABACHER. I will be looking forward to your documentation as to where that figure comes from in terms of the people that have come here illegally, rather than come in legally and overstayed their visas.

Chairman HYDE. Will the gentleman yield?

Mr. ROHRABACHER. Yes, sir.

Chairman HYDE. I have always wondered at the abuses that are inherent in the student visa situation, where I have been told we have no idea how many people are in the country by way of student visa holders who either have not gone to school—the schools do not keep records. God forbid somebody should not be able to matriculate and they get the tuition. It is just about as loose an arrangement as possible. So we have several thousand or more students who, once they are in, disappear, and I just wonder if that is too gloomy an assessment.

Mr. MOSS. Mr. Chairman, let me address that at least from the State Department side. I will get into a little bit of DHS's work, and then I would like to defer to the Inspector General.

Beginning last year, there is a very sophisticated system between the State Department and DHS called SEVIS, which is intended to track students from their visa application through their entry into the United States, through change of course, their eventual departure from the United States. And I think the Inspector General may have additional information. But I do think we have gone a long way toward dealing with the vulnerabilities that you address in the student visa program.

Mr. ERVIN. I can add only, sir, that we intend to and we will shortly begin a review of SEVIS to determine how well that system is working; and during the course of that review we will have some sense of the number of students and whether they are accounted for, whether the schools are properly accredited, whether they actually attend the schools, whether they actually depart the country when the terms of their students visas expire, et cetera.

Chairman HYDE. That will be most helpful, most useful.

Mr. ROHRABACHER. I am very happy that you intend to shortly begin the review. What we are talking about, these things are long overdue. We have experienced in this country a massive flow of illegal immigration into this country.

And I am certainly looking forward, Mr. Moss, to getting to the source saying that these people have actually come in across the borders illegally. Because, Mr. Moss, you might, when you are checking that, determine for me what the increase is in the number of legal visas that have been given to people who live in the mainland of China over the last 10 years. I understand that it is dramatic.

At the same time—I mean, people talk in California a great deal about Mexicans coming into the United States illegally, but I would contend that the major course of illegal immigration into our country today is coming from Asia, and people are coming in under visas. I would like some information as to what the number of increase in visas issued in that region are.

Finally, of the 27 visa waiver countries, do we know the number of people who have overstayed their visas and stayed here illegally, are they more from the visa waiver countries or more from people who have visas and overstay them?

Mr. ERVIN. I would say that we can't determine that because of the various problems that we have described here today, sir.

Mr. ROHRABACHER. We can't determine that because we do not have any way of determining whether someone who has come into our country illegally has returned to their home country.

Mr. ERVIN. Right.

Mr. ROHRABACHER. Well, this is incredible. Thank you very much. This has been very enlightening testimony. I appreciate you guys facing a major challenge. And we all have to work together on it. Thank you, Mr. Chairman.

Chairman HYDE. Thank you, sir. Mr. Tancredo.

Mr. TANCREDO. Thank you, Mr. Chairman. And I apologize for having been called away, because I am hoping that the questions are not redundant and I will make them brief.

When we have the new documents available and we have the new type of passport available to us, biometrically controlled, I am wondering how they will be made available. Will it only be to new applicants for passports?

And then secondly, if someone presently has a stolen passport or a fake passport and has used it many times, as has been attested to here, and evidently there is no real way of us determining whether that particular document is stolen, what would prevent them from turning that in, if in fact they are able to exchange an old passport for a new one? What would prevent them from turning one of those in for a new good one?

I guess—anyone.

Mr. MOSS. Mr. Tancredo, let me take a crack at those questions if I can. First of all, on the question of replacing old passports, we will not call U.S. passports. We have roughly 55 million in circulation. We will replace them as new applicants apply. They will receive a passport with embedded biometrics as others come up for renewal. They will be replaced with a passport with embedded biometrics.

Mr. TANCREDO. How do we know, when someone is applying for a new one, that the application is coming from someone who does not in fact presently have a false document? And that, therefore, they would get a brand new good document? You know what I mean? We are handing them a great asset if they have got a bad one.

Mr. MOSS. What I would like to talk about is how we would police that in the case of the United States passport system, and I think it is a similar system that is used elsewhere. First of all, countries have very good records on passports that have been reported as lost or stolen within their national government systems. So these records are routinely checked.

The second step is even a passport renewal is still examined closely by adjudicators in the United States or elsewhere looking for just that type of information.

I think that what you are saying is theoretically possible. I think, though, it would be very difficult for someone to pull that off, to have acquired a stolen passport and get it renewed, largely because there should be information on that old passport.

A third point, in the case of the United States, we have something called our multiple issuance verification system, which we track every passport issued to an individual. In order to get that passport replaced, in the case of my passport, Frank Moss, it would pop up on my systems, for example, that wait a minute, we have already issued three passports to Frank Moss in the last 10 years. He reported one stolen. He had that replaced. Why is he now coming in, 5 years later asking, for that one to be replaced? Oh, wait a minute; this is the number of the one that was stolen. We have a problem here.

These are the types of systems the governments frequently use to ensure the effectiveness and the security, the internal security of their passport processes.

Mr. TANCREDO. Was I mistaken in understanding from your opening comments—I did not hear subsequent questions, and I apologize again—was I mistaken when I thought I heard you say that, in fact. people are using stolen documents today, even with numbers on it, that are not being caught? That people have come in two or three times using fake passports?

How would we in fact then know? I do not get it. How would we know that they are handing us a fake passport?

Mr. ERVIN. If I could, Mr. Tancredo, it is I who said that. I was really talking about foreign passports. I wasn't talking about American passports. I would not dispute what Mr. Moss is saying about American passports and controls that are in place to ensure that a new passport, a new American passport with biometrics included, is not given to someone who attempts to exchange it for an old passport that was fraudulent.

However, that said, there is a big difference between the United States and other countries. Not all countries have a regularized system whereby, routinely, lost and stolen passport information is reported to some central location. We found, for example, with regard to France that there is not such a rigorous system of reporting stolen passport information.

Mr. TANCREDO. Oh, come on. Could that be true? Thank you. Thank you, Mr. Chairman.

Chairman HYDE. Thank you, Mr. Weller.

Mr. WELLER. Thank you, Mr. Chairman. This has been a very interesting hearing. And I appreciate the panelists participating today. Often—I should say occasionally, I have an opportunity to read publications that cater to the expatriate community, those who want to live the life of an ex pat. And I have read of certain countries that will sell you citizenship, will sell you a passport for a price. And in many cases, you do not even have to be a resident of that particular country.

And I was wondering, number one, is this true? How many countries do this? And number two, who are they? Mr. Moss?

Mr. MOSS. Thank you, Mr. Weller. There are—I can provide a more complete list for the record. There are a couple of countries around the world I can think of that have had programs that have granted nationality to someone based on an investment being made in that country. These are not countries that are in the Visa Waiver Program, sir. They are countries that, when we at the State Department become aware of it, we come down very hard on this issue because we do believe it creates vulnerabilities.

And I would just like to provide some additional information for the record on precisely what countries it is, because some countries have done it in the past, that may be what I am thinking of.

Mr. WELLER. Can you tell us who currently is providing citizenship for a price?

Mr. MOSS. Sir, I would rather provide it for the record just to make certain that what I am giving you is timely information, is not something that is overtaken by events.

Mr. WELLER. Do these countries provide someone with a passport for a fee even if they do not have citizenship?

Mr. MOSS. What they have done, sir, the couple of instances that I am aware of, they have programs for investors, people promising to make significant investments in the countries to create jobs, things like this. And in exchange for that, they have been able to acquire, on an expedited basis, nationality.

Let me check and find out exactly what countries have such programs for you.

Mr. WELLER. I would be interested in seeing the list.

Officially, what is the policy of the United States Government in regard to passports that are issued by countries which either sell their citizenship for a price or would sell an official passport for a price?

Mr. MOSS. I think in both cases the answer is the same. We undertake very strong efforts at the highest level our government, Ambassador to heads of state, things of this nature, to convince that country that they have to stop this, that they are creating vulnerabilities here, why they are creating vulnerabilities. And it is something that we routinely pursue whenever we find information about these programs and we get on it immediately.

Mr. WELLER. Do you also have figures on how many of these citizenships have been purchased by individuals or the number of passports that have been purchased by individuals from these countries?

Mr. MOSS. Sir, I don't have that data with me, but as part of the same answer on which countries have had these programs, let me see what we actually have at the State Department on the number of passports they issued pursuant to these programs okay?

Mr. WELLER. Mr. Sullivan, what is the view of Interpol regarding the sale of citizenship for a price, or the sale of official passports to someone for a fee who is not a resident or a citizen of that country?

Mr. SULLIVAN. Congressman, it is certainly something that the organization does not condone. However, Interpol, it is an interesting organization. It is really 181 different entities that are combined in a mutual group that works for the exchange of police information. One of the things that makes the organization worthwhile is to try to stay out of politics and to stick strictly with police information and the exchange of that information between countries. But I am sure under no circumstances do we condone the selling.

Mr. WELLER. You would view it as a local politics of a country to issue a passport to someone who is not even a resident of a particular nation?

Mr. SULLIVAN. I think it depends on the situation. Going back to what Mr. Moss has said, if it is a business situation and that is deemed appropriate, I would say that may be something that the organization would look at. Anytime that something like this is brought up, there is a mechanism in place that we as a country, the United States, can bring it forward to the organization and we can have the organization put pressure on that country to cease and desist with that type of action.

Mr. WELLER. Mr. Ervin.

Mr. ERVIN. I find it troubling, Mr. Weller, and as part of this review that I mentioned we can and will look at that. As a footnote as well, laying aside the issue of purchasing citizenship, as you know in certain visa waiver countries it is easier to obtain citizenship than others. Not purchases, but for the record I just want to lay out naturalization and derivative citizenship.

There are certain visa waiver countries, as you know, Denmark, Sweden, Belgium being among them, have liberal laws whereby if you are a third-country national you can come to those countries and after 3 years become a citizen of those countries. Also there is something known as derivative citizenship. Some countries have very liberal systems where in Ireland, if one of your four grandparents were Irish, you can ipso facto obtain Irish citizenship. And as we understand it, Italian law is even more liberal in this regard.

Again, it is not purchasing citizenship but it makes citizenship easier, and with regard to visa waiver countries you can see the problem with that.

Mr. WELLER. Does your Department give extra attention to passports coming from these countries, not only those who sell the passports, but those who have relatively easy citizenship requirements?

Mr. ERVIN. I can't answer that, I don't know whether the inspectors give particular attention to that. They certainly should. And that is one of the things that we will be looking at as we continue this series of reviews with regard to this complex set of issues.

Mr. WELLER. Thank you, Mr. Chairman. I thank the panel for their time.

Chairman HYDE. Thank you. Mr. Nick Smith.

Mr. SMITH. Thank you, Mr. Chairman. Several issues. What is success? What are our objectives? I would suggest that it is extremely important, whether it is the computerization or other high-tech methods, to somehow do a better job.

And let me look at the flip side of the problem. I chair the Research Subcommittee in Science, and now we see universities in other countries such as Australia, Europe, Canada and other European countries that are advertising, countries that are saying to foreign students, instead of going through all of the harassment of getting into a university in the United States, come to our universities. We are hiring the professors from universities in the United States to teach in our universities. We can give you the same science research-related experience that you could get in the United States.

I mean, that is a long way of saying that there is also a problem when you make entry so difficult for students or businessmen that in the long run, our economy loses. And that is happening in our university system. And I think it is a difficult problem. Even the SEVIS program that is designed to keep students out, to make sure that they go home after they finish their education, reduces the number of highly qualified technical students, that historically would have stayed in this country and become some of our best academic and business researchers.

I would like to hear your comments on both sides of the equation. Keeping the illegals out is important. Somehow getting an organization and tracking system is also important. I am so impressed. In my last few airline flights, I have been struck by the computerization of e-tickets. "Sorry, Mr. Smith, your plane is 20 minutes late." But what do you see as the future and the danger of systems that we are using? Are we going too far?

Mr. MOSS. Mr. Smith, I think that the points you raise are very valid ones. They are certainly ones that attract high-level attention. There are clearly working efforts underway between the Department of Homeland Security and the Department of State and the Homeland Security Council at the White House to address these issues right now.

We are trying to balance, as Secretary Powell has said, secure borders and at the same time open doors. We are a Nation of immigrants. We value the impact that foreign students have on our educational system and the value of foreign education—foreign students have on our ranks of academic researchers, scientists, what have you. We are trying to balance all of those issues.

There is an important initiative underway, and I think that some of the points you made, you will see important news about in the coming weeks on efforts that are being made to further balance these, as you very rightly put it, competing requirements.

Mr. SMITH. Got to move from that side of the equation back to the other side. Consider the 19 terrorists that came into this country, boarded the planes and attacked us on September 11th. Isn't it true that all 19 were granted visas, none came from a visa waiver country?

Mr. MOSS. That is correct, sir. And as a result of that, we have fundamentally changed our visa process. We now require face-to-face interviews. We now collect biometrics at the time of visa application. We certainly have a much expanded data sharing process among the government agencies to try to prevent such a horrific incident ever happening again.

Mr. SMITH. And that relates to the flip side where frequent business travelers and multinationals coming into this country now are complaining about having to go through a personal interview every month. We just finished an interParliamentary with Canada, and that is a special problem, being from Michigan, that we are encountering on business travel. What is being done in terms of the frequent traveler type identification to better accommodate that frequent travel?

Well, I believe that the Department is considering—the Department of Homeland Security is considering expanding the notion of trusted traveler programs throughout the entirety of the traveling regime. As you know, that system is being—or that notion is being piloted by TSA and some thought is given to expanding such system at land borders. There is the SENTRI program, et cetera. So you are essentially talking about a trusted traveler program and the Department is considering that in this context.

Mr. SMITH. I have another couple of questions, if I may. A couple of years ago we were told that the stolen passport database system was closed down on weekends, and therefore for somebody flying in from Rome—there was no way to check for them in our system. Has that glitch been corrected?

Mr. ERVIN. Our understanding is that that is not the case, sir.

Mr. MOSS. I can verify from the State Department it is a 24–7 operation. It is available around the clock.

Mr. SMITH. Anyway, gentlemen, thank you. There is no question that it is a huge challenge, but I think we have just got to be especially careful that in overprotecting ourselves we do not shoot ourselves in the foot. Half of our research in our university system now is done by foreign students. I think it is a heads-up for us to do a better job in science and math education, K through 12 and in our university system. But it also represents in the long term a great loss if we lose the kind of high-tech talent coming in from the rest of the world into this country.

Thank you, Mr. Chairman.

Chairman HYDE. Thank you, Mr. Smith. It has been reported that Ramzi Yousef who was responsible for the 1993 World Trade Center bombing entered the United States on a stolen blank Iraqi passport after first boarding a plane on a fraudulent British passport. Although we did not have the type of relations we would have needed with Iraq at the time, would the proposed or envisioned

Interpol database have been able to send necessary information on this case to us?

Mr. SULLIVAN. That comment has also been reported to me by the prosecutor who handled that case. Actually the current Assistant Secretary for Immigration and Customs Enforcement, he told me that exact fact. And I would state unequivocally that if the countries, the 181 member countries do participate in this Interpol database, that it could have been prevented and it will be prevented in the future.

I would like to echo what Congressman Smith said initially. Part of my statement, that the way that this system is going to work in the United States and throughout the world is to develop the technology, the information technology, to take the human element out of it, so that when someone comes across the border in the United States and their passport is swiped, that that database that has the stolen—and maybe in the future, blank as well as stolen—passports in it, that immediately action can be taken.

Right now, as we said before, Congressman, it is a passive system. When this is developed, when one country can talk to the other country and ping the database, that is when this system will be most effective. And I think with all the countries, when they do participate, this type of situation as Ramsey Josef, as you said, entering the United States can be prevented.

Chairman HYDE. I would hope, along with yourself, that all nations would join the database or support the global database. And so many of these problems seem to have a commonality with so many countries, maybe somebody will sponsor a world summit on passport security to iron out the differences between various countries.

I understand there are some pretty bizarre situations that are possible under the present global structure. And this seems to me a vulnerability that we have been too late in paying attention to, and I think Congress deserves some blame for that.

But you gentlemen have instructed us and illuminated the challenges that you face and that we face, and we appreciate very much the very important work that you do. And we are going to consider your statements in full and try to determine what is appropriate legislation to help meet some of these challenges. And we will be back talking to you off the record as soon as we can.

We want to thank you for your time and for your contribution. The Committee stands adjourned.

[Whereupon, at 12 o'clock p.m., the Committee was adjourned.]

# APPENDIX

## MATERIAL SUBMITTED FOR THE HEARING RECORD

RESPONSES FROM THE HONORABLE CLARK KENT ERVIN, INSPECTOR GENERAL, U.S. DEPARTMENT OF HOMELAND SECURITY, TO QUESTIONS SUBMITTED FOR THE RECORD BY THE HONORABLE THE HONORABLE JOSEPH R. PITTS, A REPRESENTATIVE IN CONGRESS FROM THE COMMONWEALTH OF PENNSYLVANIA

*Question:*

*I notice that Brunei is a member of the Visa Waiver Program. Given Brunei's neighbors (Indonesia, Malaysia, Philippines), is there any concern about terrorist cells operating in this region using passports—stolen or legitimate—from Brunei to enter the U.S.?*

*Response:*

In the course of conducting our evaluation of the Visa Waiver Program, we visited five of the participating countries: France, Belgium, the United Kingdom, Brunei, and Singapore. We chose Brunei and Singapore not only due to regional terrorism, but also because Brunei is the only VWP nation that is predominantly Muslim, and Asian alien smugglers have frequently misused Singapore's passport.

We found both countries to have highly centralized passport production with significant systems of internal controls. In Brunei, for example, the ministry responsible for passports and citizenship is also responsible for acting as the central registrar of all birth and death records, and issues all national identity cards. Centralization and reconciliation of birth and death records is an important fraud prevention tool that very few countries have implemented. As an added anti-fraud measure, the pages of each new Brunei passport are perforated at the time of issue with the bearer's national ID card number. Taken together, these controls make it difficult to imagine any non-citizen obtaining a Brunei passport from the government, or using a stolen one successfully.

The Government of Brunei is concerned that totally counterfeit documents purporting to be Brunei passports have been detected in Bangkok and elsewhere. The real Brunei passport is a highly secure document produced in Germany that contains security features that distinguish it from counterfeits. Our vulnerability to counterfeit and altered passports depends on the level of training and experience of our Port of Entry inspectors in examining such documents and utilizing their security features.

*Question:*

*In the process of adding or removing countries from the Visa Waiver Program, is any consideration given to terrorist activity in neighboring countries?*

*Response:*

Eligibility for the Visa Waiver Program has always been set in statute, beginning with the Immigration Reform and Control Act of 1986, P.L. 99–603. Conditions for joining or remaining in the VWP have been changed over the years in various immigration related bills, but terrorist activity in neighboring countries is not a statutory criterion.

*Question:*

*How are the various agencies involved in dealing with visa issues balancing the need for security with the need to ensure that deserving international students receive visas to travel to the United States to study as well as to learn about democracy? One of the most important aspects of US public diplomacy is having international students at our colleges and universities.*

*Response:*

Much additional law enforcement and intelligence data has been shared between agencies since September 11, 2001. Department of State officials have testified on several occasions about many changes to the visa application process since September 11, 2001. We defer to them to explain those changes more fully, and to describe how student visa decisions are made.

*Question:*

*If a deserving student is erroneously denied a visa, where would they go to appeal the decision?*

*Response:*

Visa applicants whose applications are denied can and do reapply, submitting additional information and hoping for a more favorable outcome. We defer to the Department of State to provide you with additional details, if desired.

---

RESPONSES FROM FRANK MOSS, DEPUTY ASSISTANT SECRETARY FOR PASSPORT SERVICES, BUREAU OF CONSULAR AFFAIRS, U.S. DEPARTMENT OF STATE, TO QUESTIONS SUBMITTED FOR THE RECORD BY THE HONORABLE THE HONORABLE JOSEPH R. PITTS, A REPRESENTATIVE IN CONGRESS FROM THE COMMONWEALTH OF PENNSYLVANIA

*Question:*

*I notice that Brunei is a member of the Visa Waiver Program. Given Brunei's neighbors (Indonesia, Malaysia, Philippines), is there any concern about terrorist cells operating in the region using passports—stolen or legitimate—from Brunei to enter the U.S.?*

*Response:*

Two countries in Southeast Asia, Brunei and Singapore, are included in the Visa Waiver Program (VWP). The continuance of these two countries, as well as 23 other countries, in the VWP is currently under review through an interagency process headed by the Department of Homeland Security. Each country review includes an assessment of terrorism both within the nominee country and outside the country both by the country's nationals and by individuals who have impersonated or might impersonate the country's nationals. The review process also examines the countries' extent of cooperation in the war on terrorism, information on lost and stolen passports, including use by nationals of other countries, the impact that VWP participation of particular countries has on U.S. national security, pertinent historical patterns or trends regarding terrorism, criminal groups, narcotics trafficking, alien smuggling, trafficking in persons, and fraud.

*Question:*

*In the process of adding or removing countries from the Visa Waiver Program, is any consideration given to terrorist activity in neighboring countries?*

*Response:*

The review process includes a comprehensive analysis of the terrorist threat posed by participating countries, including terrorist activity and potential penetration from neighboring countries.

*Question:*

*How are the various agencies involved in dealing with visa issues balancing the need for security with the need to ensure that deserving international students receive visas to travel to the United States to study as well as to learn about democracy? One of the most important aspects of US public diplomacy is having international students at our colleges and universities.*

*Response:*

There have been some significant changes to the visa process that have affected student visa applicants. Most importantly, all students must now be registered in the DHS-run Student and Exchange Visitor Information System (SEVIS) before a student or exchange visitor visa can be issued. The Department of State worked closely with DHS and U.S. universities to ensure that implementation of SEVIS went smoothly and that SEVIS did not become a barrier to timely visa processing. We believe that SEVIS has been a major improvement to border security that has not had adverse impact on student visa applicants.

In addition, virtually all applicants for student visas must now appear in person at a U.S. embassy or consulate for a visa interview. (In the past, some students could apply by mail or other means that did not entail an interview.) This change in policy is tied to implementation of the biometric visa requirement of the Enhanced Border Security and Visa Entry Reform Act of 2002. Most of our overseas posts are now issuing visas with biometric indicators that require personal appearance of the applicant in order to record finger scans of index fingers; all posts will do so by October of this year. Both the interview and biometric requirements are major steps toward more secure borders. To ensure that student visa applications are processed in a timely fashion, especially during the summer, when such applications peak, the Department has instructed all embassies and consulates to give priority to student applicants when scheduling visa interviews.

Applications from some students, especially graduate students in scientific fields, often require special clearances that include coordination with other Washington agencies. The Department has in recent months significantly shortened the clearance process and is currently involved in interagency working groups that are developing additional measures to speed and simplify the process.

*Question:*

*If a deserving student is erroneously denied a visa, where would they go to appeal the decision?*

*Response:*

Persons whose visa applications are denied have two avenues of recourse. First, they may reapply at any time and are encouraged to do so when they have new information to present, especially if the initial application was denied because of missing or incomplete documentation. Their other recourse if they feel their application was erroneously denied is to write to the chief of the nonimmigrant visa unit at the post where the visa was adjudicated. Supervisory consular officers review the decisions of line officers to ensure conformity with visa law and policies. Supervisory officers can, and do, reverse the decisions of line officers if new information is presented indicating an applicant is eligible for a visa.

LETTER ADDRESSED TO THE HONORABLE HENRY J. HYDE, A REPRESENTATIVE IN CONGRESS FROM THE STATE OF ILLINOIS, AND CHAIRMAN, COMMITTEE ON INTERNATIONAL RELATIONS, FROM THE U.S. DEPARTMENT OF JUSTICE IN RESPONSE TO FOLLOW UP QUESTIONS POSED TO JAMES M. SULLIVAN, DIRECTOR, U.S. NATIONAL CENTRAL BUREAU, INTERPOL CRIMINAL POLICE ORGANIZATION, U.S. DEPARTMENT OF JUSTICE

**U.S. Department of Justice**

Office of Legislative Affairs

Office of the Assistant Attorney General

*Washington, D.C. 20530*

July 26, 2004

The Honorable Henry Hyde
Chairman
Committee on International Relations
U.S. House of Representatives
Washington, D.C. 20515

Dear Mr. Chairman:

This responds to follow up questions posed to Mr. James Sullivan, Director, Interpol-U.S. National Central Bureau (USNCB), from the June 23, 2004, House International Relations Committee hearing entitled "Stolen Passports: A Terrorist's First Class Ticket".

In its question, the Committee noted that Brunei is a Visa Waiver country and inquired about the possible use of stolen/legitimate Brunei passports by terrorists in its region, the addition/removal of countries from the Visa Waiver Program, issuance of visas in a manner that balances the need for national security with the need to recruit deserving international students, and the appeal process for visa denials.

Brunei does not currently participate in the Interpol Stolen Travel Document Database Program. As the Visa Waver Program and the issuance or denial of passports and visas fall within the purview of the Department of State (DOS) and the Department of Homeland Security (DHS), the USNCB has no administrative responsibility in these matters and, consequently, is not in a position to provide authoritative responses regarding them. Therefore, DOS and DHS are the best sources to provide authoritative responses to the Committee's follow-up questions. The USNCB respectfully defers to DOS and DHS to respond to the Committee's follow-up questions.

Sincerely,

William E. Moschella

William E. Moschella
Assistant Attorney General

○